The Lord *is my* Shepherd

To Samuel L.R.

To my brother, Mark E. R.R.

Text by Lois Rock
Illustrations copyright © 2004 Ruth Rivers
This edition copyright © 2004 Lion Publishing

The moral rights of the author and illustrator
have been asserted

Published by
Lion Publishing plc
Mayfield House, 256 Banbury Road,
Oxford OX2 7DH, England
www.lion-publishing.co.uk
ISBN 0 7459 4859 6

First edition 2004
1 3 5 7 9 10 8 6 4 2 0

Acknowledgments
Scriptures quotations are from the Good News Bible
published by The Bible Societies/HarperCollins Publishers,
copyright © 1966, 1971, 1976, 1992 American Bible Society.

A catalogue record for this book is available
from the British Library

Typeset in 17/24 Baskerville BT
Printed and bound in Singapore

The Lord *is my* Shepherd

Lois Rock

Illustrated by Ruth Rivers

LION
Children's Books

Long ago, in the hilltop town of Bethlehem, lived a boy named David.

He was the youngest in his family, and while his brothers went off to be soldiers for the king, David stayed at home, looking after the sheep.

Out on the hillsides, he discovered the places where the grass grew lush and green.

Down in the valleys, he found where the water ran clean and clear.

He had plenty of time to sit and think.

As he sat, he practised throwing stones from his sling. He needed to be able to defend himself: sometimes a bear came prowling by; sometimes a hungry lion.

He made himself a harp from wood and string and practised playing. He made up his own tunes and sang along.

Everyone who passed by smiled to hear David sing, for his voice was clear and sweet and strong.

One day, David went to visit his soldier brothers. They and all the king's army were afraid. The enemy army had thrown down a challenge: if anyone could beat their champion soldier, then they would win the war.

But the champion soldier was a giant named Goliath. Nobody dared.

'I dare,' said David. 'I dare because I believe God will help me.'

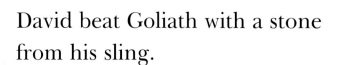

David beat Goliath with a stone from his sling.

King Saul was very pleased with
David. He became a musician in the
royal court.

He grew up to be a famous soldier
among his people, and in the end, he
became the new king.

He was rich. He was powerful. Safe in his new palace, he could compose new songs and play on the most beautiful harps.

He wanted to use all the good things he had to honour God – the One who had always protected him. He even planned to build a golden temple high on a rock in the city of Jerusalem.

It was his son, Solomon, who did the building, and when it was ready, the people needed psalms and songs to sing and play to honour God.

Among the psalms are many that David may have written himself. Here is the most famous psalm of all: a psalm written by someone who knows what it is to be a shepherd; who knows what it is to be in danger; who knows that those who trust in God will enjoy God's richest blessings.

The Lord is my shepherd;
I have everything I need.

The job of a shepherd is to look after a flock of sheep. A good shepherd must make sure the sheep have all they need.

God is like a shepherd, and God's flock are the people who listen to God's voice and want to follow God.

God will take care of them.

Dear God,

Help me to recognize the many ways you speak to me.

Help me to follow you.

Be to me a good and gentle shepherd:

always take care of me.

He lets me rest in fields of green grass
and leads me to quiet pools of fresh water.

A good shepherd will let the sheep graze in
well-watered fields where the lush green grass
is good to eat.

A good shepherd will know the places where
the rushing river waters wait for a moment,
where they curl gently in shallow pools and
the flock can drink in safety.

God knows that people need food to eat and
water to drink. God will provide for them.

Dear God,
Lead me to safe places
where the good things I need
are mine to enjoy.

He gives me new strength.
He guides me in the right paths
as he has promised.

The good shepherd will encourage
the flock as together they walk in
search of pasture, even if the way
is stony and steep.

The people who listen to God's voice will
know that God is always encouraging them
to do what is good and right.

*D*ear God,
When I am feeling strong,
help me to do what is good and right.
When I am feeling weary,
help me to do what is good and right.

Even if I go through the deepest darkness,
I will not be afraid, Lord,
for you are with me.
Your shepherd's rod and staff protect me.

The good shepherd must be watchful when darkness comes. Every sound and every shadow threatens danger to the sheep. The shepherd must use his stick to help gather them into the fold, and then stand guard, ready to defend them.

God is stronger than all the things that threaten people. God's love is stronger than death itself. God's comforting Spirit can calm the wildest fears.

*D*ear God,
I give you thanks
because you make me feel safe:
because you protect me from danger
and the fear of death.

You prepare a banquet for me,
where all my enemies can see me;
you welcome me as an honoured guest
and fill my cup to the brim.

Those who love God will know God's kindest blessings.

The day will come when the people who have been cruel to them watch in astonishment. The things that are wicked and wrong will come to nothing; the things that are good and right will flourish.

More titles from
Lion Children's Books

A Child's First Book of Prayers   *Lois Rock and Alison Jay*

Our Father in Heaven   *Lois Rock and Ruth Rivers*

Prayers to Know by Heart   *Lois Rock and John Wallace*